From Protest to Empowerment

Tee Janice,
Thank you for your
support — not only
in making this book
possible but for getting
through everything

Love,

Joe "Kommon
Knowledge"

From Protest to Empowerment

MANIFESTO X & O

Kommon Knowledge

iUniverse, Inc.
New York   Bloomington

From Protest to Empowerment

Manifesto X & O

iUniverse books may be ordered through booksellers or by contacting:

iUniverse
1663 Liberty Drive
Bloomington, IN 47403
www.iuniverse.com
1-800-Authors (1-800-288-4677)

ISBN: 978-1-4401-0768-9 (pbk)
ISBN: 978-1-4401-0769-6 (ebk)

Printed in the United States of America

iUniverse rev. date: 11/25/2008

Jade Andrea,
our ancestors prayed that they might
endure their exploitation and oppression.
God answered by giving US you and your kind.

Contents

Foreword

Poetry speaks to the heart and soul of a matter. It tells the naked truth and breaks down walls and barriers. It makes you think, cry, and laugh.

Poetry speaks of God and it gives voice to the righteous, rebellious brothers...and sisters. It paints a picture of justice and freedom and it bemoans the unfairness of political and societal ideologies.

And...it's all about passion.

As I get to know Kommon Knowledge, it's obvious he's a brother with a cause that's driven by his passion for change, for fairness, and for justice. The power in his words will grip you because they're tight. They not only squeeze your heart, but they squeeze your mind, as well. There is also power in his literary prose, which speaks to our consciousness and makes us aware of the revolution.

He is a true revolutionary!

But what is a revolutionary? It can be defined as one who engages in a revolution; one who constitutes or brings about a major or fundamental change.

In his own words, the revolution he speaks of is not about tearing down, but, instead, about turning around. He seeks not to revolt, but to revolve, to find solutions and resolve. I attest to the fact that in his writings, Kommon Knowledge is one who advocates, adheres to, and actively gives voice to fundamental changes in the thinking of society.

He's told us once before, and he now reminds us, the revolution has certainly begun.

Taya Hargrove
author, *Every Time I Close My Eyes*

Preface

"Hold on, my People!" Eddie Kendricks was singing that to US back in 1972. Ironically, WE still heard Erykah Badu singing that in 2008.

It seems that the saying has been somewhat of a mantra for my people as WE endure generations of suffering and struggling throughout our American experience.

By saying WE, I not only make reference to the oppressed and exploited masses of the United States in general but more specifically to her Black citizenry; the racial group to which I happen to belong. But some obvious questions may be *what are WE holding on for* and *how much longer are WE going to have to hold on?*

WE are holding on for a change; an improvement in our social condition. However, what WE need to understand is that WE did not get into our current social condition here in present-day America by happenstance.

Omali Yeshitela of the African Peoples' Socialist Party blamed a post-feudalist Europe as it moved towards colonization and imperialism throughout the world. According to him, "The capitalist world economy was born as a consequence of what Marx called the primitive accumulation of capital." To this end, many of US believe that our current social condition is a direct result of being brought here as slaves to labor for the gains of capitalism and from having remained enslaved in America for generations.

I make no apologies for speaking out on our social condition in this book. Like James Baldwin said, "I love America more than any country in the world and, exactly for this reason, I insist on the right to criticize her perpetually." The same Constitution that has facilitated and fostered our social condition into being also permits me to voice my opinions. My inalienable right to free speech is a constitutional guarantee which allows me to express my disdain and contempt for the establishment and its systems. And so, I do this bearing the comportments of Huey P. Newton, Assata Shakur, Theodore Kaczynski, Mumia Abu Jamal, Bill Ayers, Malcolm X, and countless others who have dared to be demonstrative in their dissatisfaction with the status quo. See, James Baldwin also told US, "To be a Negro in this country and to be relatively conscious is to be in a rage almost all the time."

In concurrence with Bob Avakian of the Revolutionary Communist Party, "it is only those with nothing to lose but their chains who can be the backbone of a struggle to actually overthrow this system and create a new system that will put an end to the exploitation and help pave the way to a whole new world."

Finding slavery at the root cause of our social condition, I underscore that WE were not enslaved in America by happenstance. In fact, our enslavement is even prophesized in several places in the Bible. To illustrate, the Book of Genesis 15:13-14 states, "And HE said unto Abraham, 'know of a surety that thy seed shall be a stranger in a land that is not theirs and shall serve them; and they shall afflict them 400 years; also that nation to whom they shall be in bondage will I judge,' said God. 'And after that shall they come forth and serve me in this place.'" As does the Book of Acts 7:6-7 which also states, "And God spoke of this wise, that His seed should sojourn in a strange land; and that they should bring them into bondage and entreat them evil for 400 years. 'And the nation to whom they shall be in bondage will I judge,' said God. 'And after that shall they come forth and serve me in this place.'"

Our 400 year period of enslavement began with the arrival of the first African slaves here on America's shores circa 1619. With the slavery continuing up to the present-day, Biblical prophesy has been only being fulfilled. See, WE suffered through some 246 years of the atrocities of human chattel slavery before its legal abolishment. Then for more than 140 years since slavery has become illegal, WE have had to live with an erroneous sort of freedom that has been intertwined in Black Codes, systems of peonage, unfair sharecropping practices, Jim Crow segregation, corrupt convict leasing programs, unjust treatment in the criminal justice system, and extremely discriminatory redlining policies. Throughout our enslavement my people have gone from rural plantations, farms, and fields to defunct factories in urban slums and ghettoes with many of US ending up in prisons and penitentiaries along the way. As of today, however, our prophesized 400 year enslavement has been nearly carried out and WE must be prepared for what comes next.

Presently complicating matters is a pseudo-type of bondage that exists largely within the minds of my people and which coexists alongside some covert vestiges from many of the post-slavery policies and practices mentioned earlier. Evidence of this can be seen within many of the behaviors of Black folks in our communities. While many of these instinctive, adapted behaviors are a testament to our resilience, resourcefulness, and ingenuity as a people enduring the conditions of our enslavement here in America, other behaviors that WE have adapted for our survival are destructive and of great detriment to US as a nation of Black folks. The behaviors to which I refer have included our perpetuation of underground economies such as illegal gambling or the selling of illicit drugs to our people, our consumption of certain foods that contain little or no nutritional value, our lack of self knowledge, and our inability to connect with our ancestral lineage in Africa, to name a few. To add, these detrimental behaviors have my people leading in the number of incarcerations nationally. There is also an abundance of single parented households that are headed by women in our communities. Moreover, WE have much higher rates of acute and chronic health conditions running across multiple generations in our families. In addition, absentee fatherhood amongst my people is widespread and rampant. Furthermore, throughout the years since legal slavery has ended, my people have failed to acquire the sort of wealth that can be passed on from one generation to the next on a large scale.

Dr. Manning Marable cites "the millions of African-American families forcibly separated through sale; the generations of Black slaves coerced to build university buildings, courthouses, banks, and railroads without compensation; the nameless millions denied access to higher education, employment, and access to health care under the intolerable regime of Jim Crow segregation" as part of the explanation. Moreover, things have gotten this way and have largely remained the same for so long because WE have been just holding on for all of this time; doing whatever WE have had to do in order to survive. In agreement with the premise of Joy Degruy Leary, PhD., our behaviors and attitudes were adapted for our survival during slavery and the adaptations continue to manifest today. To date, America has not yet fully acknowledged the impact that slavery has had on US and she has done little to make amends. Therefore, no atonement has truly been made for her wrong doings.

However, our time for change has come. The end of our enslavement is near and a game plan is required; a veritable manifesto of the x's and o's that WE need to follow so that WE can come forth in this land and do as the prophets have foretold.

As WE Proceed: A Movement for the People was written to help US peep the game and the theory behind the game. My intent was to get people thinking and talking; critical thought being the antecedent to action. In proceeding onward and forward, *From Protest to Empowerment: Manifesto X & O* has been written in an attempt to lay the foundation for the game plan. A manifesto being the formulation of a condemnation on systems and the establishment, x's and o's allude to the mapping out of offensive and defensive strategies employed by athletic coaches and their teams. My hope is that our game plan will come as a result of people critically thinking about the content and meaning of these poems and from increased dialogue on these matters afflicting the proletariat.

In our lifetime WE have seen governments topple, kingdoms crumble, economic systems fail, and traditional social orders abandoned. America has moved from having an economy based on agriculture and industry where the labor has been largely exploited, to an economy that is based on technology and becoming increasingly global in scope. There is evidence of an impending change on our horizon. World-wide social unrest is looming and the masses of American people are getting restless as well. People are becoming demonstrative in their dissatisfaction with the status quo and the establishment is uneasy because they can feel their grip beginning to slip.

In keeping with what has been prophesized, WE know that a change is going to come. Hold on, my People …

In the meantime, visit **myspace.com/aquestcalledknowledge** to engage in continued dialogue and critical thought as WE formulate a game plan.

I Am … I Can

Do WE have equal air time
for Barack Obama,
baby mamas,
and Osama?

False media
has US seeing the
sensationalism that equals dollar signs
as maniacs shoot up Columbine high schools
and Virginia Tech college campuses.
Like addicts shooting up on illicit substances.
What is this?!?
The injustices
of an unjust, never ending war.
Blame games and
political games;
playing pawns with our poor,
disenfranchised,
underemployed,
and uneducated.
WE underestimated.
An understatement
of the tears that fall
as fears rise
'til it rains from our cries for freedom.
All of US can hear them
but WE still don't believe them.
A Black man
with nothing to lose
has nothing to prove.
Nothing to lose but his chains …
Nothing to prove except that he can change …
Nothing to change
except the game.
See, there was no change from the trial of Denmark Vesey

to the case between Ferguson versus Plessey.
Seemingly no change
from The Book of Genesis
to the case of the Jena 6.
So, WE need our roots and culture
chiseled deeply into US like sculptures
in the same guise
as these same guys:
Nat Turner
Medgar Evers
James Baldwin
Steven Biko
Sonny Carson
Amiri Baraka
Who is your hero, negro?
See, lacking knowledge of self conceals
what history will reveal.
I am.
I can.
And I always have been
but ignorance and misunderstanding
made me not know what was happening.
Like the proverbial tree fallen
in a deserted forest,
which does make a sound
but the People have to be around to hear it.
Commonalities in our ancestral spirits
are still questing that which WE seek.
In the spirit of the Prophet Muhammad, I speak,
with knowledge ranging
from quoting biblical
to ranting political
as highly critical issues weigh-in as pivotal
on news outlets
and multi-media conglomerates
as Osama gets
his equal time

to broadcast videos
and speak his mind.
But if my brother falls in the ghetto
despite no one being around
doesn't he still make a sound?

Acts 7:6 And God spoke on this wise, That **His seed should sojourn** in a strange land; and that they should bring them into bondage, and entreat [them] evil **four hundred years.** 7 And the **nation to whom they shall be in bondage will I judge,** said God: and after that shall they come forth, and

WE Raise the Flag

WE raise the flag
for US colored folks;
so colorful.
RED,
BLACK,
and GREEN!
As WE wave these colors
for our sisters and brothers,
WE represent in strength
the tribes of our African descendents.
The ankh symbolizes our key of life.
Like *Songs from the Key of Life,*
WE live just enough for the city
with just enough pity
to survive through the stress
and the strife
of what WE feel.
Feeling as cold as black steel
and chaos bringing
our final call for Black power
in the eleventh hour.

As WE raise the flag,
highly critical and overblown
are conspiracies
and plots of political regimes overthrown;
bringing a corrupt government's tyranny
and reign down
to face Hell and damnation.
Raining down like hail
on this damn nation
as some have chosen that almighty dollar
over Almighty Allah.

WE raise the flag,

with a false media as critical
of political figures
brought back as political prisoners
from exile
to stand trial
but only to get railroaded.
They have our jails loaded
with Latinos and Blacks
as Conservatives attack
a poor, disenfranchised societal underclass
pinned down and held underneath a glass ceiling.
Revealing a game theory
that WE should plainly see.

Yes, WE raise the flag
for US colored folks;
so colorful.
RED, BLACK, and GREEN!

(1NE 14Z) Out Past Curfew

In just this past week,
following a homicidal game of hide-n-seek,
another day found
another adolescent body chalked off on the playground
as the homicides hide by night.
From our urban eyes' sight,
WE witness crimes committed on urbanized sites.
That is what some say.
But why is it called "gun play"
when guns fight
as the homicides hide by night?
Finding an urban plight
in partial paralysis
being the price paid
for peddling crack …
a bullet lodged within his back …
in between the 9th and 10th vertebrae …
WE heard them say,
"He may never walk right again."
And then …
wheelchairs that wobble
and young boys who hobble
like old men with canes
shot up over selling 'caine …
Got puppet strings on the trigger so who pulls it?
Who shoots the anonymous bullets?
Out of the blood saturated Timbs
come amputated limbs …
rehabilitation …
prosthetics …
perhaps a halt to a promising career in athletics
or just being able to play around
while pee-wees pour out liquor on playgrounds
as stray shots
spray blocks

and shots at corner stores
begin wars
between children who are trying to survive;
hell-bent on remaining alive
as the homicides hide by night.

Daily Urban Dramatizations

Even in the ghettoes,
there are professionals
just like there are hoodlums
amongst the chaos and the bedlam.
There are also dope fiends
shooting up and smoking
those weapons of mass destruction.
Key factors of mass consumption
and key factors in the commission of suicide.
Like do or die,
"Red Tops go two for five"
making mass commerce
without the commercials.
Just daily rehearsals
of urban drama
played out
without delay.
Without screenplays.
Without scripts or cameras.
Just amateurs
and innocent bystanders
standing by
awaiting the revolution to be televised.

By Nominal Nomenclature

What is in a name?
HE,
ME,
or WE?
Its all the same.
As WE proceed, HE remains
our Alpha and Omega
in a world without an end.
Anno Domini Nostri Iesu Christi Amen.

My People Gotta Listen

In vacant back lots
adjacent to crack spots
where 9mm guns go bust
and bums cuss,
as some fuss about
government subsidies
suddenly taken out.
Suddenly WE got to make it without.
Went from Section 8
up to paying rent at market rate
but with no increase
in income.
Just more problems for some.
But what is it that keeps
the People from listening to me?
Is it plain old ignorance
or paranoia from conspiracy
on the profits gained
playing a prophet's game?
See, even with me
there was a skeptical sort of cynicism
'til I decided not to fight it.
And I realized
the potential provided
as "untied" becomes "united"
with knowledge,
wisdom,
and understanding.
But perhaps it is in their planning
because for some it seems
unforeseen
to do for self.
But then they'd rather ask you help?!?
Instead of embracing economic self-sufficiency
by any means, to have a life lived sufficiently.

Government subsidies suddenly taken out. Suddenly WE got to make it without. Went from Section 8 up to paying rent at market rate but with no increase in income.

Faux Gazin' Fulgazis

WE be faux gazin'
folks with names ranging
from some of those
in neosoul,
or borghe
to Bohemian.
Some even claiming
to be artists of the spoken word
but all you ever heard
were spoken words.
No rhythm.
No rhyme.
No reason.
Seems like its open season
for dead poets
who don't even know it;
who had not expected
to be resurrected
and then
murdered an art form all over again.
Claiming to be
"keeping it real"
but yet and still
just fake as fuck.
Or you week-end dreds;
substitute,
poor excuse
to be weed heads
who claim to be freer
than the mind of Mumia
but both body and soul
are all out of control.
Crying happy tears.
Some got nappy beards
longer than Bin Laden

but they been hiding
behind so-called movements
not knowing what they are doing.
Also naming them
pseudo-ghetto soldiers
and revolutionary posers
put out by a false media exposure
as so-called revolutionaries
who got all "brand new".
And you
RED, BLACK, and GREEN wearing,
claimed to be God fearing,
wearing ankhs,
and cowry shells,
and beads having
on African medallions;
Like trying to rock
on top with a multi-colored kufi;
not cultured but goofy.
Or even
an uneven Afro.
Unnatural.
Not a struggle
for the rights of the People
because they struggle for the single
and for the rights to mix and mingle.
And those of you
who put on head wraps
then head back
to your coffee houses
early evening
'til late night.
It ain't right.
As WE see
social movements
subconsciously
being held back by

the self conscience
and egos
of certain 9 to 6
socio-political activists.
Like so called movements
are being held back by
the so called
socially conscious
fulgazis
as WE be faux gazin'.

In Jena Louisiana during 2006, a Black student sat under a tree in the schoolyard where only White students sat. The next day three nooses were hanging from the tree. As racial tensions mounted, a fight took place in which a white student was beaten and suffered a concussion and multiple bruises. Six Black high school students were charged with attempted murder and they faced up to 100 years in prison without parole.

<u>Jena 6: Verse 4</u>

Jim Crow applauds
its so-called
southern hospitality.
In reality,
a modus operandi
of murder,
mayhem,
and mishap.
Then this hap.
The Jena 6.
Young brothers in a fix.
It has me wondering
on the subjugated subtleties
like if from southern trees
there hangs
this Black-skinned fruit that is strange
then why doesn't his blood
make the grass grow
into underground movements
on grassroots levels
deep enough
to disrupt the Devil
as he runs lose
while given just enough rope
to get hung
in his own noose?

Get 'Em Up

My People, do y'all realize what happens
when WE get all five fingers folded into the palms of our hands???
Goddamn!!!
Can't y'all understand?!?

An expression of our militant Blackness
is the raised Black fist.
As WE resist
by making a fist
and WE begin pounding it
against the complexity of our problems
compounded with
ignorance and confusion
confounded by illusion.

But revolution
provides the solution
to our problems.
So, my People, let US go out and solve them.

Brothers and sisters, take your fists and get 'em up!
Get 'Em Up!!!
Get 'Em Up!!!

666

Corporations,
politicians,
and prisons.
Amerikkka is a 3 headed beast marked by 666.
Putting our nation at risk
are Dummycrats and also Republican'ts.
The American public gets into trouble and
the People try to do what is right
only to end up dealing with what is left;
just winging it.
As government censorship attempts to kill the noise
but our protests keep bringing it.
Revisiting
Supreme Court decisions
and dissenting Justice opinions
envisioning
justice denied by sell-outs;
Those Clarence Thomas-like negroes
need to get the hell out.
Those fork-tongued, 3 headed snakes
need to be burned at the stakes.
The President,
our Supreme Courts,
and our Congress!
WE brave a political power-play
playing on the fears of the American people.
Like COINTELPRO was aimed to counter terrorist,
public policy shaped opinion just because WE got scared of it.
But is this the Land of the Brave?
Or the Land of the Afraid
with our ignorance feeding the egos
of Amerikkka's 3 headed eagles?
Or is the bird like the proverbial phoenix
that rises from the ashes
as those ashes get swept under the rug again

by the Democrats and Republicans?
And George Bush, Sr. once led the CIA,
so, you can see why they
will use surveillance,
counter intelligence,
and espionage
unless WE grow eyes
in the backs of our heads.
Allowing US to hide
our revolution from 33 1/3 of their eyes in the sky.
Because an electronic, glass eye may be all-seeing
but after being
misquoted
and replayed
out of context
on MSNBC,
seeing ain't always believing.
Making it seem odd that
some Republican'ts switch back
to being Dummycrats.
Knowing that some folks on the left
just ain't quite right.

Hallo WE En

There is no time for wasting
on celebrating a pagan holiday;
no time to play.
WE got work to do.
WE got Klansmen
masquerading as policemen.
Some in uniform and others in plain clothes
but they all need to be disrobed.
So, instead of hitting the streets
looking for a trick or a treat,
WE need to be out in those streets
pulling off their sheets!

Rev Or End

Some of US marched in DC just to be a part of something.
Others believed that it could be the start of something.

But back home WE got this council of Black Baptist ministers
acting sinister,
seedy,
and straight out greedy.
In cahoots and making covenants
with the business community and local governments
then singing, "WE shall overcome …"
and chanting, "Let US march on
'til victory is won."
But how long will it be
'til WE truly are one?

The post-industrial blight of urban America

CRIME SCENE DUE DI

0 122869 ??????? 8

WR1T3 0N MY BR0TH3R5 4ND 5I5T3R5

Profit-sized

Building on our past
as WE travel our paths just
like the Prophet Saul on the road to Damascus.
Knowing that only a fool will walk
where wise men seldom wander.
So, small wonder, as fools rushed in
and in a rush to judgment
WE bum-rushed in
as Operation Desert Storm
when it should have been operated by brainstorm.
Now the opportunity costs increase
as our opportunities to live decrease
because the so-called costs of living in peace
are placed beside an asterisk.
Replaced as the risk
as WE separated the drama.
WE separate it by a comma
and WE take the words WE wrote
and put them inside of quotes.
Then WE make our point-
marked by an exclamation
of AK47 and M16 gunfire.
It comes down to the wire
as a mass exodus.
Exit US yelling,
"Burn baby, burn!"
and making heads turn.
But it is just US
calling for justice
and causing this raucous.
When WE put our heads together
into a veritable
ghetto think tank
WE peep games
and peep crimes:

Black on Black ...
White collar ...
Blue collar ...
The American government got US folks by the collar
and held down under her thumb.
Playing US as if WE are dumb.
Like WE cannot see
folks getting rich off of this war
being fought by the poor.
While out on the block,
young boys do dirt;
out there putting in work.
And those boys out on the corner,
WE may no longer know them
but it is still up to US to go out and to show them
that greed is destroying our world
and poverty is the real weapon of mass destruction;
a direct result of over-consumption.
How long can WE ignore
as horror came
along with hurricanes,
earthquakes,
tornadoes,
and tsunamis?!?
Global warming
or a global warning
written in our ranting,
our rages,
and our rampages?
This is prophecy that goes on for pages and pages.
Profit-sized as just right for Ecclesiastical pimping
but packaged as what was prophesized as simply
the post-industrial blight of urban America.
Knowing that God is eternal.
His truth is universal.
Meanwhile, supporting our aggression
and economically supporting the oppression

of ourselves and our offspring
by paying our tithes and our offerings
as WE still find it hard to sleep
out on inner city streets
paved with
blood on the pavement;
bled from the have-nots.
Those that have-got American privilege
dismiss the dilemma as frivolous.
Like Michael Eric Dyson debating poverty
with Bill Cosby.
Obviously, getting US nowhere.
But why even go there
because of the Black-Whats,
the Black-Ifs,
and the Black-Maybes?
Could it be because of crack???
May be.
Plus WE got babies
being raised by babies
that are having babies
and some of them are addicted to crack
but, of course, WE already knew that.
Plus, it is 3 strikes and out
with mandatory sentencing for crimes
committed for the third time.
Plus WE got over-zealous cops
handing out speed knots
to hard-headed niggas who heed not
and continue selling drugs out of designated weed spots.
A modern-day showdown
as some of US get shot down
and beat down by rogue police
who need only to be exposed to cease.
Whether on dashboard cameras
or video taped by amateurs.
While caught on tape

trying to escape
are criminals
and suspects
and innocent bystanders.
But some are backed by blue
and they stand behind badges.
There are also smear campaign tactics
employed by the establishment
like entrapment.
The lesson there?
Learn to separate the message from the messenger.
Then, with a unified voice of the people,
WE will never be separated and unequal
no more so than WE will ever be silenced
so long as WE arise speaking volumes
through our potential to become violent.
See, it is nothing more than prophecy
as the critics of ghetto prophets be
preferring that storefronts get smashed and burned down
instead of investing some cash and turning things around.
Just philosophically waxing prophetic
on the state of our union because it is pathetic.
But WE upset the balance
when the status quo gets challenged
by US hustling,
struggling,
striving,
and surviving
Middle Passages and atrocities,
ironically, to face the holocaust of slavery,
Jim Crow segregation,
and now disenfranchisement
plus under-funded education
along with a class struggle that is conflicted
and babies being born crack-addicted
or with fetal alcohol syndrome.
All underneath a Constitution that ain't worth the paper it is printed on.

See, my People, it has all been profit-sized
with drug dealers guilty of committing homicide,
dope fiends committing suicide,
and the American government guilty of genocide.

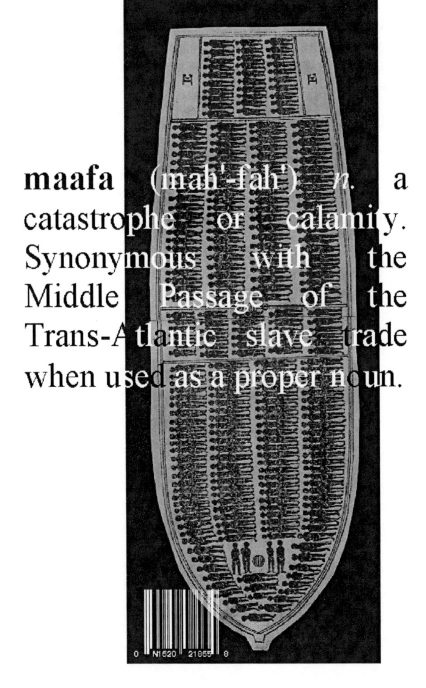

maafa (mah'-fah') *n.* a catastrophe or calamity. Synonymous with the Middle Passage of the Trans-Atlantic slave trade when used as a proper noun.

Trade

WE can trace the Atlantic trade winds
to way back before when
a trans-Atlantic slave trade begins;
where the exchange for culture and trade
made above the Sahara,
sub-Sahara,
and West Africa
a regional center for trade
in 13th century
Ghana and Mali
and Songhai empires
until 1492; prior
to European greed and desire
for exploitation
under the auspices of exploration.

Still Strange Fruit

How many fathers and sons
will WE continue to be robbed of
as their nooses are still hung
and from what the lynch mob does?
Because hung from tree limbs
like fruit stems
were the snapped necks
of lynched Black men;
Hanging there like some strange fruit
dripping blood at the root
of trees in the Deep South.

In 1973 the Independent Oglala Sioux Nation seized the Pine Ridge Reservation as part of the armed resistance of the American Indian Movement.

Shared Reservations

I have traveled down the other side of the mountain a time or two.
And I have driven down through
North Carolina.
That is where you will find the
Cherokee Indian reservation.
But from my observation
it was no different than Black folks' housing projects
with the same complacency due to our common lack of prospects
and the same lack of prosperity
that accompanies poverty
and the realities
found in the commonalities
of our shared reservations and regrets.
It tells US of those tales of tears
that were left on the Trail of Tears
by tribes like the Creek,
the Seminole,
and the Cherokee
who were cheated by treaty
out of their lands in Georgia, North Carolina, and Tennessee
when The Indian Removal Act was passed in 1830 during
the presidencies of Andrew Jackson and Martin Van Buren.
Given a rubber stamp
to concentrate Native Americans into camps
and to keep them under lock and key
by the United States Calvary
on executive orders
to steal their land and add to our borders
while waiting to march them out west to Oklahoma.
But by 1890 in South Dakota,
Sitting Bull would war with General Custer

at the Battle of Wounded Knee;
a turning point in American history
marked by struggle and resistance
and abandoning any hopes of having a peaceful coexistence.
Proving that our Red-skinned sisters and brothers
are no different than any other
of US folks whose skin is Black or Brown
when it comes to getting down
with revolution.

New Millennia Nigga

If niggas are so scared of revolution
then who is out there doing the shootin'?
Can it possibly be
some of those
universal negroes
who try to be
everybody's everything
but ain't really being
nobody's anything
nor anybody's nothing?
Because what WE find troubling
is that along the evolutionary continuum
within this new millennium,
are some real *e*-negroes
and *i*-niggas
who still can refer to each other as "my niggas".
And while it may be true that
niggas are scared of revolution,
I ask you
who are these real negroes,
really?

Somos El Mundo

"Jose can't 'chu see
by the dawn's early light
what WE loudly called Hell
at the twilight's last gleaming?"

Pero el gente del mi barrio
son Norteños
y Sureños Mexicanos
o Chicanos.

Otros son Cubanos.

Mi familia somos Puertoriquenos.
Boricua o
Taíno y Africano.

Si, yo soy el Rey del Mundo
y todo el mundo es mio.
Vaya contigo
as WE proudly proclaim to the world,
"Nosotros somos
Afro Ricanos"
with a bit of Conquistador
and some blood from the ocean explorers
like Cristobal Colon.

Revolution Has Been On TV

The system is too much for US to handle.
WE got to change the channel!
WE keep watching channel zero
waiting for another hero
or savior to save US.
WE keep watching channel zero
with nothing on our minds;
wasting time.
WE keep watching channel zero
with nothing on our brains,
so, it is insane
to expect something different.
My brothers and sisters, what is it?!?
Why won't WE just change the channel???

Ghetto Soldiers

Pouring out like libations
onto the curb wasting
is our ghetto soldiers' blood
as it floods
from gunshot wounds and veins
then down into sewers and storm drains.
But WE don't get equal TV air time
to cover that crime.
Despite the news media exposure,
our ghetto soldiers
don't get flag draped coffins on the 6pm news;
they just get over-opinionated editorials and views
from Conservatives calling for stiffer penalties.
While the war in Iraq is the one that WE see
our American soldiers dying.
Yet government censorship is still hiding
their flag draped coffins.
So, WE must wonder how often
does this happen in the war
that WE ignore?

On November 16, 2007, tens of thousands gathered in Washington, DC to protest the U.S. Department of Justice's failure to prosecute a series of hate crimes across the nation.

Jericho a-Tumblin'

Can you hear the trumpets sound?
Can't you hear the sounds of injustice crumbling?
Throughout the halls of the Justice Department there is a rumbling.
Seven times WE marched around
and, just like Jericho, the walls came a-tumblin'

                                         d

                                          o

                                           w

                                          n.

So, take heed as the trumpets call
signaling that the modern Jericho is bound to fall.
Look out y'all 'cause the walls are a-tumbling!!!

Foolish Convictions

He was a convicted dope fiend
who went about hoping
that no one would find out.
"Brothers gonna work it out!"
Like he used to front
on our clenched raised fists,
our revolution,
and our calls for BLACK POWER.
But did his dope on the side,
sold crack,
or pushed the white powder.
Got put on lockdown
from petty crimes
and a drug habit.
Then dropped a dime
on the Movement,
so, someone let him have it.
He sold out his soul
to the Devil.
Back on the streets
and got some drugs in him.
But they found him stuck
up in the cut
with a slug in him.

What 15
the price for the
life
of 4 veteran?

STR8 2

THE UNITED STATES OF AMERICA

h3LL

7734

3X4M1N1NG 50M3 0F TH3 H4RD NUM83R5

(What about ME?) US?

If America can't afford
to provide healthcare for her citizens dying from AIDS,
then how can WE spend billions of our tax dollars
in humanitarian packages and foreign aid?!?

Like a two-faced American Eagle,
choosing the lesser of two evils
means that you are still choosing evil.
And the World Bank,
International Monetary Fund,
and international banking cartels,
along with the people running this land
all got blood on their hands.
So, what is the price
for the life of a veteran?
Perhaps, in terms of today,
nothing more than a slave
because WE send in our troops
to tear off the roof
then turn around and spend billions
on good will and nation building.
With the U.S. government up to no good.
Out of money to spend right here in the 'hood.
Gross National Debt used to enslave me
but no money to even save our babies
unless a social condition gets labeled as epidemic
which means that they could no longer contain it
in places where some will say
that some still play
childhood games of cops and niggas.
Based upon the data from the figures,
the facts and the stats,
our contents remain under constant pressure
because WE all share a common oppressor.

But if America can't afford
to provide healthcare for her citizens dying from AIDS,
then how can she spend billions of our tax dollars
in humanitarian packages and foreign aid?!?

Although millions may get confused
from the fucked up news on FOX and CNN,
among the People it has been
scribed like archaic cuneiform
or the ancient hieroglyphs
in the wild-styled graffiti and tags
on rusted iron or steel and broken glass.
The cracked concrete
of once glamorous citadels
that now lie in veritable ruins
as seen in Jerusalem.
Reminiscent of Rome,
Thebes and Athens
but now what merely has-been
from the former glory days
of a golden age
in places like Philadelphia,
Chicago, Baltimore, and Detroit.
Successions in urban blight
and suburban flight
as WE abandon, and gentrify, then exploit.
Which also can be seen
down there in New Orleans
because they referred to Hurricane Katrina evacuees
as refugees but not as American citizens
and sat back claiming innocence over ignorance.

So, if America can't afford
to provide healthcare for her citizens dying from AIDS,
then how can WE spend billions of our tax dollars
in humanitarian packages and foreign aid?!?

T3CHN1C-All Difficulties

Multimedia exposure
misshaped our culture
from early ages spent on Sesame Streets
where WE learned to read
ABCs,
NBCs,
and CBSs.
WE see the messes
made of printed news
on newsprint.
But no one knew
that the news went
from offset printing presses,
to internet blogs and web addresses,
AM talk shows,
satellite radio,
podcasts,
and cable television broadcasts;
a continuous mass media bombardment
leading US to a mass brainwashing.
Put the FCC on trial
and don't touch that dial.
But will WE stay tuned
and stay doomed
despite the technical difficulties?
False media- WE don't need it, do WE?

Bastard Sons & Daughters

As WE relinquished our freedom to speak
in return for having the freedom to believe in what WE got told
by a Congress that got paid for, bought, and sold
and WE became like children of a slain father;
His bastard sons and daughters
living in defiance of God's will.
"Thou shalt not kill."
But our evils committed abroad along
with our covert warfare ventured upon
led to the retaliatory attacks
on the World Trade Center
and Pentagon.
Despite the Japanese bringing it straight to US at Pearl Harbor,
WE still did not even bother to take heed.
In order to put an end to the tyranny,
do unto others and just let them be.

4CKN0W73DG3, 4M3ND, 4ND 4T0N3

Armed with knowledge,
wisdom,
and understanding,
WE can then begin demanding
an absolute truth
that is rooted in our hypotheses
on the scriptural prophecies.

For the Movement,
the People,
and the Vanguard
as WE stand guard
with our weapons locked and loaded
in refutation
of US being considered refugees in this nation.
Our Civil Rights struggle teaches US a lesson.
Perhaps WE all must be prepared to pick up a weapon
or keep steppin' and put down the Dream-
or so it may seem.
So, out goes the calls
for quiet and calm
when the wrong-doers do wrong.
And out goes their calls
for blue walls of police
who do not stand there at ease;
nor in parade rest
wearing Kevlar vests
and full riot gear.
Once again, there will be no quiet here.
Just hillbillies with billy-clubs.
Push comes to shove
when killer cops create cop killers
out on inner city blocks
as some even cop from the drug dealers
while WE yell out, "No justice- no peace!"
and then shout, "No racist police!"

However, divided WE stand
as a nation fallen on denial.
Like the nation fallen on the Nile
described in the scriptures,
America stands exposed by me
as a modern-day slave holding society.
And too much profiting
has left the People out here begging.
But our prophets shall continue counting down to Armageddon
for a redemption that is marked in blood
and flowing as deeply as the waters of the Great Flood.
Meanwhile, an age old divide and conquer strategy
has our People parting like the Red Sea
leaving US departed like the dead be
and talking only from a distance-
like the African drums be.
Still, somehow, only some see
that WE may play follow the leader
wearing A-One jimmies and wife beaters,
doo-rags,
and over-sized jeans that sag.
But putting the Dream down doesn't mean that WE abandon it;
WE just become more wary of whom WE are standing with
like those who are casually dismissive
of White privilege as frivolous.
Exposing game theories and corruption on all levels
committed by blonde haired, blue-eyed devils
who turn states evidence
then fade into obscurity as if their crimes were irrelevant.
And in between the lines of the media lies the truth
behind the deployment of NATO armed peace keeping troops.
Yet WE, the People, get demonized by the media;
an unduly dehumanization
as seen through the demon eyes of our nation.
Green with jealousy and envious.
They envy US for the law passages
that Congress writes as rubber checks for balances

of our rights and their wrong-doings.
While in Iraq, Iran, and Afghanistan,
folks like Johnny Taliban
and other disenchanted Americans
take up arms and fight
along embattled, war-torn frontlines
that somehow get pushed off the front page
and torn out the headlines.
Scores of American soldiers
who have embraced Islamic culture
somewhat similar
as the Knights Templar
did with Emperor Saladin and the Assassins.
See, from Tehran to Tel Aviv,
in fields filled with poppy seeds,
the sell of heroine
is what really finances the terrorism.
While the other side uses weapons of mass distraction
to commit the crime of grand theft oil.
But until the plot is foiled,
it only breeds our skepticism
as the shroud of secrecy for the plot uplifts.
It leads US towards the Apocalypse.
Perhaps, the Book of Revelations provides the sequel-
an end to a world filled with tyranny and evil.
Because whether they are war crimes,
Black on Black crimes,
or crimes committed by white collar,
it seems that WE are out here chasing a dollar
with financial woes
that take their tolls,
so, WE should have seen it come.
Like the war in Vietnam,
an unjust war in the Middle East
only fosters terrorism instead of peace.

For the fruits of her evils and sins,
America must acknowledge, atone, and amend.

TH353 73TT3R5 4750 H4V3 NUM83R5 BUT 0N7Y 50M3 OF U5 C4N R34D TH3M.

4M3R1C4 0NC3 W45 4 GR8 N4T10N.

4M3R1C4 MU5T 4CKN0W73DG3 H3R D33D5 4ND 4CC3PT R35P0N51B171TY. TH3N SH3 MU5T B3G1N 2 4M3ND H3R W4Y5 SO TH4T 4TON3M3NT M4Y B3COM3 4 P0551B171TY.

W3 N33D 4 D3M0CR4T1C 4RM 0F 50C14715M B4 1T5 2 78.

FR33D0M 4ND 4MN35TY 2 TH3 M0V3 9, TH3 4NG074 3, MUMI4 4BU J4M47, SUND14T4 4C071, G3R0N1M0 J1 J4G4, 4554T4 5H4KUR, B0B 4V4K14N, TH30D0R3 K45CZ1N5KY, 53K0U 0D1NG4, K471M4 45W4D, 4BDU7 M4J1D, 4ND 2 477 P071T1C47 PR150N3R5 OR TH053 0N 3X173.

K0MM0N KN0W73DG3 H4T...N

0 NUM83R5 73TT3R5 8

<u>Prophe See</u>

It has been spoken on
through the prophecies
from the Watts Prophets
to the Last Poets,
Gil Scott-Heron,
Curtis Mayfield,
Marvin Gaye,
and Isaac Hayes.
WE revel off of the revelations
from Reverend Jesse Jackson's and Al Sharpton's
sharp tongues.
And WE ponder the ghetto prophecies
of Notorious B.I.G.
and Tupac
on the jukebox
as there is also prophecy in the lyrics
of Jimi Hendrix
and Bob Marley.
So Mister Charlie,
when WE turn on the news
and sing our Monday morning blues,
the prophets of Yahweh Elohim-
Ibrahim,
Isaac,
and Yacob,
have taught US to survive and to make it.

4 Little Children

It is amazing how little children
play in vacant lots and boarded up buildings
where an old box spring
becomes a trampoline.
Trampling
discarded needles,
broken crack vials,
and social class denials.
Along with popsicles sticks and lollipops
are stray shots that loudly POP!
                                    POP!
                                    POP!
And while a drug addicted mother turns tricks,
her child turns flips.

(WE Got) Somethin' Goin' On

WE got somethin' goin' on; the evil doers are still goin' strong.

My People, dig me.
This ain't the 1960's,
but WE can still die
by the ballot
as well as the bullet
because too ready to pull it
are sell-out niggas
with one hand on the trigger
and the other hand in a voting booth
withholding the truth
and too willing to sell their soul
for the falsehoods
and promises
of something that glitters like gold.
Bought, paid for, and sold.
Like supply and demand,
the lies and deception go hand in hand
with political corruption;
where one dirty hand washes the other clean.
No consistency.
Unfamiliarity with the constituency
becomes a well-known scheme
for a politician that is seldom seen
after WE have already voted, so,
the low man on the totem pole
gets acknowledged even less
or altogether polished off at best.

WE got somethin' goin' on; the evil doers are still goin' strong.

WE got somethin' goin' on … WE got somethin' goin' on.

(Conquering Lying) Lion 4 Lambs

If America could birth a "rogue nation" when the Shah of Iran dies,
then Blacks can be arrested without being properly Mirandized.
While playing the game of follow the leader
may seem to be easier until we realize
that WE also follow the lies of the leader.
See, WE only seem to remember what has been said
once our Black leaders are left lying dead
and our mothers are left at home crying
over lambs sent out to their slaughter amongst the lions.
Engaged in war in the Middle East
or right out here in these streets
as veteran soldiers
of illegitimate wars
are merely given Purple Hearts
for giving up their body parts.
WE play pawns in this game
by the Devil and his Federals.
Meanwhile, failed and failing policies
on the U.S. and global market economies
have the People out here hurting
despite how hard WE are working.
In fact, it seems WE have never worked harder
to close a poverty gap that seems to be opening farther
between the haves and the have-nots;
eliminating the middle class
by taking from US what WE ain't got.
Our government's political schemes are half-cocked;
and the People just get double crossed!
Left out of the urban economic equation
and then lied to by the leaders of our nation
whether from war crimes committed in Iraq
or crimes committed by Blacks against Blacks
because the colors life, liberty, and freedom are GREEN!
You know what I mean?
And so, WE get caught up all too often

And left to rot inside of the Devil's coffins-
his jails and institutions.
Perhaps, the Afrikan Holocaust is Amerikkka's Final Solution.

WEmerge

As our Black leaders emerged,
many of US were urged
to harness our anger.
Despite the dangers,
they devised strategies
to challenge injustices
and to organize
making it possible for US to arise
by standing up,
filing lawsuits,
marching,
and protesting
as a more unified voice.
Speaking up for those of US
who had been voiceless.
Yes, our Black leaders emerged and they made choices
to dare dream of days without injustice.

The Greatest of American She-roes

She escaped from slavery
and then bravely
risked life,
limb,
and liberty
while being bounty hunted
and despite being wanted
dead or alive,
she returned and led more than 300 slaves to survive
their bondage
and she managed
to help them find freedom
through networks of Underground Railroads.
Harriet Tubman,
truly the greatest of American She-roes
and the "Moses of her People".

Black Women

Remember, you have been impeded by a glass ceiling
and invisible barriers
that are often scoffed about and disputed
in terms of their physical existence
but still, an all too real hindrance
to enjoying the fruits of your labors.

Instead, Black Women, you have pacified yourselves
and denied yourselves.
Struggling and sacrificing;
by any means, surviving
as the backbones of our Black families.
Such strong matriarchs within a white-dominated, patriarchal society.

Despite your beliefs,
some of your sons are sacrificed to the streets
while your daughters are raised to hold down families of their own
once they become full grown.

But now as America calls,
she has the gumption and gall
to ask you to cast your vote neither by race or by gender
while ignoring her political agenda?!?

heshima (heh-shee-mah')
n. respect, honor, or deference taught to children from an early age

<u>Hey Huey</u>

In the spirit of neopantherism,
WE call the People to achieve a renewed sense of activism ...
    BLACK
    Power through
    Academia and
    Nationalism by
    Teaching US knowledge of self and
    Heritage so that WE may begin building sufficient
    Economics to fund as well as to form a continued
    Revolution giving all power to the People.

Our Fathers

WE lost legacies
as our fathers failed
at fatherhood
and then fell farther
from the 'hood
through the paternal lineage
and the patronage
of the pimpin' papi
making babies
with a baby mama
while making drama
out of daddy's maybes,
mama's babies,
and more legacies lost.
Descendant of this,
our daddies WE missed
and WE continue to pay the costs.

America is ... RED, WHITE, & BLUE

America is ...
blue collared,
White supremacist,
red-necked,
and badly in need of a head check.
As WE wipe our weeping eyes
blood-shot red
with knuckles worn white
and weary
from being wary
of blonde hair,
blue eyes,
and Black compromise.
America is ...
the absence of some much needed head room
that causes blood-red head wounds
split down to the white meat
by her true blue lynch mobs
and even thinner, bluer lines of rogue cops.
America is ...
Bleach-whitened wife beaters
and white tees,
red doo-rags
or blue bandanas,
Chuck Taylors and blue jeans
on bodies that lie lifeless at crime scenes.
America is ...
red, white, and blue-in-the-face
from breathing in white hot fumes
that get blew in her face
as she fans the red, hot flames of revolution
ignited as media falsehoods are
read, write, and blew out of proportion
beyond the point of distortion
like white noise levels

that red-line loudly
made by blue-eyed devils.
America is …
US Black folks sadly singing the Blues
about the realities and the rules
from that good ole boy, red-blooded
White American privilege.
America is …
racist and frivolous.
America is …
a nation fallen down
with racism conspiracy theories that abound
from her blueprints
for widely read headlines
that get white-washed for the American public;
just a sorted bunch of hogwash
for US to get smothered in.
America is …

Red Carpets Roll

They can pretend to roll out the red carpet
as if WE are royalty
but what has my blood boiling
is that all WE normally get is shut down,
locked out,
and blocked up
like our dollars ain't green.
Know what I mean?
So, instead of taking our money to spend with them,
WE need to be boycotting and putting an end to them.

Divide & Conquer

The media uses some common buzz-words
like cuss words;
a veritable name play.
Like some tug of war game played.
Empowered by when they say:

      extremist …
      oppositional …
      militant …
      radical …
      subversive …
      insurgency …

because its all a divide and conquer strategy.
And critics may call me "a **radical**, pro-Black Nationalist,
wearing an Afro that can be considered **extremist**,
fanatically preaching some **oppositional** shit"
but it only hides the corrupt politicians' missions
to further divide and conquer US
by robbin' 'hoods.
Like Robin Hoods
who steal from the poor and give it to the rich-
now ain't that a bitch?!?
And when WE separate
the Church and State,
what WE really create
is a great debate
and an even greater divide
as WE provide the provisions
used to make the decisions
between the haves,
the have-nots,
the go-getters,
and the ain't-gots
while maintaining their divisions.
See, united WE stand but divided WE fall
yet at times WE are all

divided along race
and divided amongst faith.
Peep game:
a Black mind that is strung out on crack
committing crimes against Blacks
is also contributing to genocide
but somehow it all gets rationalized
as do or die;
a survival of the fittest
due to flawed logic that is irrational.
The rationale is to separate by need,
separate by greed,
separate by wealth,
or to separate by what WE believe.
Jah Rastas,
La Raza,
El Rukns,
and Muslims
WE seem to agree that Abraham, Jesus, and Muhammad were all prophets.
So, perhaps a motive for the divisiveness lies within the profits
of fostering and hosting an unjust, unholy war.
As for the African Diaspora,
like a scattering of seeds
thrown into the breeze,
a crime should never be
Black on Black.
Self hatred, loathsome attacks
committed in this manner is suicide.
So, when WE choose sides,
the absolute truth is only used to divide
and conquer the People.

Y'heard ME?

Say, brother, have you heard?
Thirty three and one-third is the word.
As if Masonic ritual were involved
WE, the People, revolve
'round and 'round and 'round.
Like a 12 inch single spinning
'til the ending comes back 'round to the beginning.
And as prophesy foretold the rebirth of a nation
WE, the People, witness the fall of the kingdom of Satan.
His high-rise tenements are falling as did the Tower of Babel.
But my brothers and sisters are still herded like cattle
into low-income housing projects
and left without hope and even lower prospects
for the next two or three generations.
The same can be found on American Indian reservations.
Plus, haven't you heard the news?
Section 8 is now being used
to concentrate US poor folks
with no reservations.

TH3 P30P735 M0V3M3NT: 4 QU3ST C4773D KN0W73DG3

<u>The Dope Fiend Lean</u>

Peculiar,
that it seems to be so familiar-
the way that a dope fiend leans
towards the realm of illicit drug use
and illegal substance abuse.
Although, it fries the brain,
still, others will come and try the same;
by any means, to get the drugs in them.
From the first injection of that poisonous venom
intravenously
WE BEGIN COMMITING SUICIDE
heinously
until one day
where WE may be found
face down
powdered nose to the ground
in the snow.
And left out there with no place to go.

Black Children

WE are the pain,
the shame,
and the burden
that lasts a lifetime from a childhood of hurting.

WE are the bi-product of four or five fatherless generations.

The world's greatest industrialized nation
has left herself a legacy of collateral damage
in single Black mothers finding some way to manage
day to day finances.
Heading households,
dodging dicks,
and providing for welfare and health
while failing to generate generational wealth.

That, too, becomes collateralized
as the damages go so much farther
than just being Black Children without fathers.

BL4CK_F4M1LY

4 Colored Separation

As WE raise the flag
waving the colors of Black Nationalism,
RED, BLACK, and GREEN
is what WE give them.
But somewhat fewer
somehow knew the
RED, GOLD, and GREEN
from the flag
for the Kingdom of Judah.

Manifesto X & O

A manifesto formulates a condemnation
on systems
and the establishment;
the very foundations of this nation.

But it is made manifest first in the mind.

Abusing and misusing
a U.S. Constitution.
Not written in ink on parchment
so much as it has been soaked in our blood
on West African mudcloth
then rubbed off,
blurred,
stirred,
and distorted,
twisted up and contorted
into a mutated system of justice.
How can any of US trust it
when the Office of the Presidency
and the Joint Chiefs
don't want peace.
Pulling a perpetual bait and switch.
They get US to discuss, debate, and then switch
the issues and our channeled energy.
Get US tuned-in on an irrelevant frequency
Like Black Maybes
or whatever the shade of Black de jour may be-
from pro-Black or just
not Black enough
or somehow Blacker than thou
with our parades rained on by black clouds
as others remain Black and proud.
While conservative-minded motherfuckers talk shit
claiming that crack babies are a myth

and that the over-prosecution of Blacks doesn't really exist.
Disregarding Black Maybes
as Whats and Ifs
but what if WE were to consider
that the Devil's standard
provides a double standard
for the People who truly know
which way the wind blows
and how the weather is underground.
See, Vietnam was a proven undoing for the Black family
Fast forwarding 40 years is like rewinding to the very same calamity
of conflict in Iraq; another exploitation
executed by the Great Satan.
With judges to bribe
and politicians to buy,
special interests have got the system by the pocket
backed by warheads, missiles, and nuclear rockets.
And beware of those moving in the shadow of Wall Street.
Like corrupt politicians, they are also called thieves.
In return, they may call me
an enemy of the establishment,
a conspiracy theorist,
or an alarmist.
But the People are getting more fed up
as WE fill up
and with our resentment rising
as our attitudes boil
over the rising price of Arabian oil.
And if WE take it to the streets,
the ones in riot gear will be the police.
Just like an endorsement
with unquestioned law enforcement
in favor of the establishment.
So, WE hold in contempt again
the European banking system
and World Trade Organization
because they foster globalization.

Its like our Constitutional rights held back by barbed wire
while the government-controlled media conspires.
But rather than waiting for prisons or coffins,
the game plan is laid for our defense and offense
within a manifesto of x's and o's
to take back what is actually owed.

In Cogs WE Trust

In God WE trust
but its been made scandalous
and more crooked than the corrupt politicians caught trickin'
then shuckin', jivin', and boot-lickin'.
As WE follow the lead of folks with no soul;
the ones in control researching alchemy and occult symbology
then reforming science, religion, art, and philosophy.
Characterized by Ted Kaczynski,
as "mere cogs in the social machine"
while our soldiers are paid for and sold,
then sent off to war but not returned to US whole.
With a CIA-sanctioned coup d'état
as the coup de grâce.
Giving rise to the protests of anarchists,
sympathizing with the Communists,
and using leftist activism
by means of social radicalism.
WE oppose the exploits of the prison industry
and the Universal Product Code as the mark of the beast
with subliminal marketing and psychological tactics given
backed by the corruption of the capitalist system.
Disenfranchised as a People,
WE come demanding
knowledge, wisdom, and understanding
of truth and for some exposure
to the legacy of our roots and culture.

The ?uestions

What are they so scared of?
Perhaps it is because I have Black skin.

Some may scoff at the notion and laugh, so,
maybe what they fear is my afro.
Or is it my 6 foot frame?
Could it be my name?
Is it the way that I question the system?
Do they wonder whether I belong in a prison?
Is it a fear of my beliefs?
Or a fear that my education also comes from the streets?
What are they so scared of?
Perhaps it is because
I have Black skin.

Amen Khamin

The rivers of blood
from our children flow and flood
like the field of Akel Dama.
Violence and drama
feeds their seeds
and then branches out like trees.
See, WE managed to build a mess
more epic than Gilgamesh.
Created a world full of young folk
who often act but do not know
of themselves, or of their culture, nor religion;
breeding amongst them ignorance and suspicion.
When the truth is that WE are a race of gods and earths;
the mighty offspring of the universe.
But it is like selling the Greeks, Phoenicians,
and Egyptians on monotheism.
As it has been written,
Gaining One's Definition
is to merely admit,
"I submit Lord and master."

Never 4get

Flash, rubble, and fire
tumbled the tower
of the world's last super-power
in a deadly storm
of steel,
stone,
glass,
and ash
that rained down
when it came down.
Like twin brothers built
with commerce, greed, and guilt.
Ahura Mazda and Ahriman
in the lore of the Zoroastrians;
a towering ziggurat over the Modern Babylon.
As WE proceed to babble on
about the evil deeds that men make
seeming to purify the landscape
but with a death toll that is unknown.
Archangel Gabriel's trumpet calls the soldiers home
among the innocents who find Heaven
and martyrdom on 9/11.
Upon a hallowed ground zero,
America has found her heroes
and an abundance of theories
on the conspiracies
that are still shrouded in secrecy
in our minds and made to enter
on the fate of the World Trade Center.
With a corrupt government, the media cover-up begins.
Like the Kennedy assassination all over again.
So, WE ring the alarm as Satan continues to conspire
for world supremacy and his global empire.

<u>80 D</u>

The greatest industrialized nation
is increasing her rate of incarceration for young folks.

America- all high and mighty
and over represented by Whitey.
She has pushed the Red man onto her reservations
and shipped in the Black man to slave on her plantations
while using the Yellow man to build her railroads.
Rewriting our exploitation out of their historic tale told.
Baffling the board of education
because young folks get so bored of education
when its difficult for them to make their own connections.
What they need is our redirection
because for entertainment
some entertain with the deadliest games of cops versus niggas.
Check the stats.
The facts and figures show our young ones losing interest like the Dow Jones.
Thinking that most of the great Black leaders are now gone.
And so WE must sing a song
for our sister Assata,
and for brothers like Sundiata,
Geronimo ji Jaga,
John Africa,
and Mumia Abu Jamal
who took a stand and gave all;
fought and sacrificed
for our better quality of life.

But unless WE show this,
our young folks won't know this.

2 Skeptics & Narcoleptics

Some of US have conscience
but with a socially unconscious take
while walking around presumably wide awake
with the game fully peeped
on so-called enlightened folks
with a 3rd eye
that is sleep.
Others are blind, dumb, and deaf.
So, who amongst US will be left
to hear the *Distant Thunder*
and then begin to wonder
about the ties between the UPC
and the mark of the beast
or a Novus Ordo Seclorum
beholden to secret societies?
To share some thoughts on violence,
freedom,
and urgent means?
Or to debate exactly what *"Rising Down"* means?
Using our native tongues,
WE must call forth our young
and then WE must begin
to prepare them.

DM

RATED DANGEROUS MIND

UNDER 10 YEARS OF AGE AND WRITING WITHOUT ADULT
SUPERVISION

APPROPRIATE SUBJECT MATTER FOR ALL AGES

Epilogue

By writing this book, I am not seeking deification as some sort of contemporary urban griot. Nor am I even claiming to have any answers, per se. More so, my hope remains to increase the amount of critical thought that the People are having and to foster dialogue on the matters that crucially afflict US so that WE can collectively devise our game plan.

During casual discourse with my own child, she informed me that *her third eye was wide open*. Hearing her say this absolutely floored me! See, when I think about my childhood and how carefree I lived back then and how oblivious I was to our plight, it amazes ME to see children nowadays who are in tune with the struggle. However, I do realize the importance of the place that children have within the Movement, its Vanguard, and even in its leadership. Case in point, Mumia Abu Jamal had already been targeted by the government as a key member in the Black Panther Party by young age of 15.

Perhaps it cannot be said better than Psalms 72:4, "May HE vindicate the afflicted of the people, save the children of the needy, and crush the oppressor." That is to say, no revolution can be complete if it does not include our children. The revolution did not begin with US but as long as there is oppression and exploitation WE need to become conscious to the fact that it must continue. And so, I leave you to dwell upon the following ...

The War No One Needed

Why did WE die
in the war no one needed?
And why did WE kill the innocent
in the war no one needed?
Why did the terrorist start
the war no one needed?
Why did WE blow up Iraq
in the war no one needed?
To answer my questions would be a miracle
about the war no one needed.

Jade
author, *age 9*